LANDMARKS OF
BRITAIN

LISA PRITCHARD

MYRIAD BOOKS

Westminster

For the British, the single word "Westminster" encompasses the parliamentary establishment. The Palace of Westminster (above) is the home of both the House of Commons and the House of Lords.

The eastern end of the palace is dominated by the Clock Tower with its great bell, Big Ben. The combined length of the "corridors of power" and rather less important passages in the maze-like palace is more than 2 miles (3km).

Just across the Thames from the Houses of Parliament, the London Eye opened in March 2000. The Eye is suspended over the river, with A-frame legs grounded on the south bank. Step aboard one of the 32 "pods" on a clear day and for the next 30 minutes you will be sure of some of the best views of London. When the weather is at its best you can see for 25 miles (40km) in each direction.

Westminster Abbey

A stone's throw away from Parliament stands Westminster Abbey (above), the focal point for many national events from coronations to royal weddings and state funerals. This is a place of pilgrimage for many as some of the nation's key poets, musicians, writers and politicians are buried here.

Outside in Parliament Square statues commemorate major figures in Britain's political life, including Benjamin Disraeli, Robert Peel and Britain's wartime prime minister Sir Winston Churchill – a towering influence in the first half of the 20th century, many still consider him to be Britain's greatest politician. It is a short walk across Parliament Square and down Whitehall to Downing Street.

Trafalgar Square

The northern side of Trafalgar Square is dominated by the National Gallery, home to one of the world's premier collections of European paintings, with masterpieces such as the *Madonna of the Pinks*. Curiously, this is also where the UK's imperial measurements of length (inches, feet and yards) are literally set in stone, under the balustrade.

Every year Nelson's Column has to compete with an enormous Christmas tree in Trafalgar Square, a gift from the people of Norway to thank the British for helping to liberate them at the end of the Second World War. It's an uplifting sight throughout December, the beautiful tree and the illuminated fountains playing.

Come January Nelson's Column (left) and his four bronze lions return to centre stage. Massive classical sculptures are mounted on three of the four plinths on the square. The fourth plinth currently showcases modern sculptures for six months at a time.

Buckingham Palace

When George III bought the Duke of Buckingham's townhouse (left) in 1761, it was simply one of the Royal Family's many houses. His flamboyant son George IV (1820-30) commissioned John Nash to redesign the building but died before it was finished. His brother William IV, rather unenthusiastic about the project, offered Buckingham Palace to Parliament after fire destroyed the Palace of Westminster in 1835. But Parliament refused and rebuilt Westminster instead. Two years later Queen Victoria made Buckingham Palace her official residence. Today the palace doubles as the head office of the monarchy and the Queen's home. In June each year the Queen marks her official birthday at the Trooping of the Colour ceremony (right) in Horseguards' Parade.

Tower Bridge

Tower Bridge (right) was opened in 1894 to service the expanding business area in the East End of London. Its central span splits into two sections that are raised to allow tall vessels to pass through to the port facilities upriver in the Port of London; it still opens about 600 times a year. Visitors can view London from the raised walkway.

Tower of London

London's ancient fortress, the Tower of London (below), is one of the capital's key tourist attractions, renowned for the Crown Jewels, the Yeomen Warders (Beefeaters) and its imposing stone towers. The White Tower was built by the Normans. In the Middle Ages the Tower of London was a royal residence, but in Tudor times it became a notorious prison. Those who fell from grace, such as Henry VIII's wives Anne Boleyn and Catherine Howard, arrived by river at the Traitor's Gate. Few survived – most were incarcerated in one of the towers and later executed. The walls of the Beauchamp Tower still bear inscriptions etched by prisoners all too aware of their destiny.

St Paul's Cathedral

Sir Christopher Wren oversaw the rebuilding of more than 50 churches in the City of London, lost in the Great Fire of 1666. His first design for the new cathedral was based on a Greek cross, with four equal arms, but Church Commissioners insisted on the traditional Latin cross, with a long nave and short transepts.

Thirty-five years after building work began, the 79-year-old architect saw his vision completed. You can walk up the 259 steps to the Whispering Gallery inside the dome: if you whisper to the wall, someone standing on the opposite side will hear you clearly. The Stone and Golden Galleries offer panoramic views of London.

Felix Mendelssohn once played the organ here. It is housed in an intricate case by the woodcarver Grinling Gibbons, and has 7,189 pipes and 138 stops.

Globe Theatre

The new Globe owes its existence to Sam Wanamaker, the American actor-director. His long campaign to rebuild Shakespeare's Globe was a triumph, and the theatre opened in 1997. It is an historically accurate replica, complete with thatched roof, an open-air auditorium, lime plaster walls and wooden galleries. When it opened both the public and theatre critics greeted it with scepticism, but it has since become one of the most successful theatres in Europe.

Tate Modern *(above)* and Tate Britain *(left)*

Henry Tate made his fortune by refining sugar. He gave his huge collection of Victorian art to the nation, and paid for the first Tate Gallery at Millbank. Regional galleries in Liverpool (1988) and St Ives (1993) were followed by the addition of a bold new gallery at London's Bankside power station, now named Tate Modern. The collection is divided into British and Modern art – the original gallery, Tate Britain, shows British art from 1500 to the present, while Tate Modern houses Modern art from 1900 to the present day. Tate Britain runs the Turner Prize, an annual competition for artists under 50.

Royal Albert Hall

The home of the summer season of BBC Proms concerts, as well as countless other performances, the Royal Albert Hall is a grand building, erected as a result of the Great Exhibition of 1851. The sum of £200,000 was spent to build it "for the Advancement of the Arts and Sciences, and works of industry of all nations, in fulfilment of the intentions of Albert, Prince Consort". Its bold iron and glass dome rises to 835ft (275m) and it seats over 5,200 people.

Albert Memorial

On the other side of Kensington Gore stands the Albert Memorial (above), raised by Queen Victoria in memory of her beloved husband. Completed in 1876, it was designed by the eminent architect Sir Gilbert Scott.

South Kensington museums

The cluster of museums along Cromwell Road in Kensington largely owe their existence to Prince Albert's grand scheme, the Great Exhibition of 1851.

The Victoria and Albert Museum (above), better known as the V&A, is renowned for its collections of paintings and sculpture, especially early Italian works. Here you will find Canova's *Three Graces*, and Raphael's cartoons for the tapestries in the Sistine Chapel. The wide-ranging collections of some four million items include glass, textiles, ceramics and jewellery.

Step through the imposing entrance of the nearby Natural History Museum (left) and you are immediately faced with a huge *Diplodocus* skeleton in the Central Hall, a stunning introduction to the museum's collection of fossilised dinosaur skeletons and a favourite with younger visitors. The museum's 70 million items take a long view of Earth's animal, plant and mineral riches.

Science Museum

Tucked behind the Natural History Museum is the Science Museum (left). A very popular destination for children, it vividly shows the impact of science in shaping modern life and offers fantastic hands-on workshops and demonstrations that may literally make your hair stand on end. The museum has its own Imax cinema, which features 3-D films on space exploration and science.

Greenwich

The home of Greenwich Mean Time and the Prime Meridian line, Greenwich has played a pivotal role in the history of science. This World Heritage Site consists of the Old Royal Observatory, the Queen's House and the Royal Naval College (right). Designed by Sir Christopher Wren, the Naval College was built "for the relief and support of seamen and their dependents and for the improvement of navigation". From 1873 to 1998 the elegant building housed the Royal Naval College, and today it is shared by the University of Greenwich and Trinity College of Music. The tea clipper *Cutty Sark* (below) sits in dry dock by the river at the heart of Greenwich. Now a museum ship, it was launched in 1869.

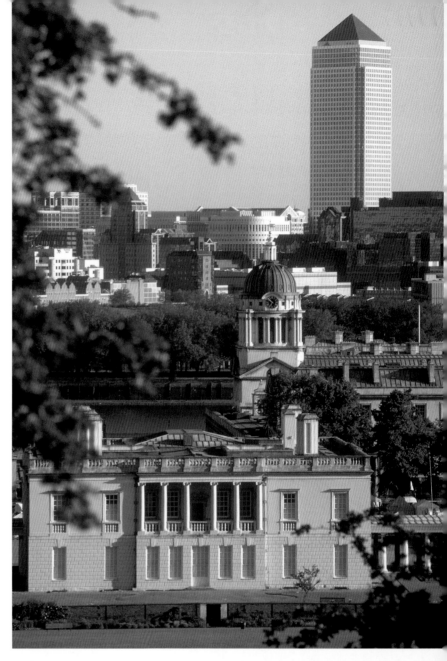

Kew Gardens

Kew Gardens has spectacular displays of flowering plants and shrubs. Equally dramatic are the 19th and 20th-century glasshouses, which provide perfect microclimates for tropical and subtropical plants. Decimus Burton designed the huge Temperate House (right), the largest Victorian glass structure still standing. In 1987 the Princess of Wales Conservatory (above) was opened. Much of the space is underground, with 10 computer-controlled environments, to cater for plants from extreme desert conditions to dense, humid rainforests.

Hampton Court

This was Henry VIII's favourite
palace, and he added the Great Hall
as well as the Real Tennis courts.
In 1689 Sir Christopher Wren
remodelled the King's and Queen's
apartments. The most famous feature
of the gardens is the hedge maze,
with more than half a mile
of paths. Elsewhere avenues laid
out by William III radiate from the
house, through 60 acres of formal
parterres and "wilderness" gardens
along the river Thames. Visitors today
can see the Tudor kitchens and the
state apartments, and stroll in the
courtyards and gardens.

Windsor Castle

Perched on a hill in the centre of
Windsor, a bustling town on the
banks of the Thames, the castle has
been inhabited for 900 years. St
George's Chapel, within the castle
grounds, dates from 1475. It is the
home of the Order of the Garter, the
highest order of chivalry the Queen
can bestow. Henry VIII and Charles I
are among the monarchs buried in
the chapel, as are the Queen Mother
and the Queen's younger sister,
Princess Margaret, who died in 2002.

Canterbury

Canterbury was already an important city in the Middle Ages: the seat of the Archbishop of Canterbury and a staging post between London and the south coast. The Norman cathedral still towers over the city today. Henry II's bitter dispute with his Archbishop of Canterbury, Thomas Becket, lasted eight years. Becket refused to acknowledge the state's supremacy over the church. In 1170 Henry's men murdered the Archbishop in the cathedral. Pilgrims flocked to his tomb, inspiring Chaucer's *Canterbury Tales*. Beside Becket is the tomb of Edward III's son, the Black Prince (below), a key figure in England's battles with France in the 14th century.

Beachy Head

On a clear day there are truly stunning views from the top of Britain's highest chalk sea cliff, Beachy Head (580ft/162m). Eastwards lies Eastbourne and Hastings. To the west you can see Newhaven and Brighton, and sometimes it is even possible to glimpse the Isle of Wight.

The lighthouse was originally built 540ft (165m) out from the base of the cliffs, but in 1999 a huge chunk of the cliffs slipped down into the sea, and now the land almost reaches to its foot. Stretching away from Beachy Head, the rounded Seven Sisters cliffs have been a crucial landmark for sailors for centuries.

Dover Castle

The white cliffs tower over the port of Dover, forming part of the North Downs, and visible for miles. The Roman lighthouse still stands on the clifftop, as does Dover Castle. From the Normans to the 20th century, the castle remained strategically important.

Miles of tunnels inside the soft chalk and black flint of the cliff provided barracks during the Napoleonic Wars, and were used as an underground military command centre and hospital during the evacuation of Dunkirk in the Second World War.

South Downs

The South Downs run for about 70 miles (100km) across the south of England from Eastbourne in Sussex to Winchester in Hampshire. A popular trail, the South Downs Way, follows this ridge of chalk downland, much of which is an area of outstanding natural beauty.

Six miles north-west of Eastbourne stands the Long Man of Wilmington (left) on Windover Hill. The first known drawing of this 227ft (69m) figure dates back to 1710, but nobody really knows when it was first etched into the hillside.

The view from Ditchling Beacon, 3.5 miles (6km) north of Brighton, is rightly famous. This is the highest point in Sussex, and was one of a chain of beacons where bonfires were lit to signal an attack.

Another attraction in the area is Glyndebourne. Opera buffs flock to the annual summer season as they have since 1934. Tradition demands a champagne picnic in the grounds during the interval.

The Solent

This sheltered stretch of water separates the Isle of Wight from the British mainland. It is a busy waterway: as well as ferries bustling across to the Isle of Wight and the occasional passing of Royal Navy vessels, it teems with yachts of all kinds especially during Cowes Week in August every year.

The Solent made Portsmouth the ideal port for a seafaring nation. Families still gather on the Round Tower (right) to wave goodbye to sailors on board Royal Navy ships as they sail out from the harbour. In 1545 Henry VIII watched his great flagship the *Mary Rose* sink here as she sailed into battle against the French.

A somewhat happier destiny brought *HMS Victory* (below) to dry dock in Portsmouth. Admiral Nelson's flagship is the world's oldest commissioned warship. It is both the flagship of the current Second Sea Lord and a living museum of the Georgian navy.

The Needles

At the western end of the Isle of Wight stand the Needles, a series of chalk stacks, which seem to march out to sea. They are quite stubby – the formation was named after a needle-shaped column that stood in the middle until storms caused its collapse in 1764. On the outermost rock sits the unmanned Needles Lighthouse. When Queen Victoria and Prince Albert began to spend their summers at Osborne House near Cowes the island became very fashionable. Cowes' August sailing regatta and the Isle of Wight music festival attract thousands of visitors every year.

Winchester

Winchester, where modern cricket began and the novelist Jane Austen is buried, was once the capital of King Alfred the Great's kingdom of Wessex. With the rise of London, Winchester remained an important centre for learning and religious affairs.

To stand in the Cathedral Close when Winchester Cathedral's 14 bells are rung is simply breathtaking. Thirty-five English kings were crowned here, and 20 of them buried, including King Canute. St Swithin was Bishop of Winchester in the 9th century: legend has it that rain on St Swithin's Day (July 15) means rain for the next 40 days.

When Oliver Cromwell demolished Winchester Castle he kept the vaulted Great Hall (left) for assemblies and County Assizes. In pride of place hangs a huge 14th-century table, rumoured for centuries to have been the Round Table of the legendary King Arthur and his famous knights. Today the county town of Hampshire prides itself on good food and a lively arts and crafts scene.

Stonehenge

The origins of Stonehenge are shrouded in mystery. Was it a giant astronomical observatory, or a sacred burial site? And how did primitive people transport these huge stones and set them into the ground so that they are still in position 4,000 years later? This megalithic stone circle was clearly an astounding feat of engineering. When the sun rises on equinox and solstice mornings its rays stream through the gaps in the stones. Stonehenge still inspires awe even in the most cynical observer today.

Salisbury Cathedral

The soaring beauty of Salisbury Cathedral (right) remains a wonder of 13th-century craftsmanship. The spire, completed a generation later in 1333, is the tallest in Britain. Inside is the oldest working clock in Europe, dating from 1386, as well as one of the four surviving original versions of the Magna Carta, signed by King John at Runnymede in 1215.

Dartmoor

The bleak splendour of Dartmoor's granite outcrops and boggy moorland stretches across a great swathe of the West Country. Dartmoor has more than 160 high rocky hills known as tors. A perfect example is Combestone Tor (above) which overlooks the valley of the river Dart. Perhaps the most popular of all is Hay Tor in east Dartmoor. Its fine granite was mined in the 19th century for buildings such as the British Museum and the old London Bridge. Every year 2,500 young people take part in the gruelling two-day Ten Tors race.

Land's End

The westernmost tip of mainland Britain is on the Penwith peninsula, near Penzance in Cornwall. While Land's End is a popular tourist destination, its name is most often heard in connection with sponsored fundraising attempts to walk, run or cycle the full length of Britain from Land's End in the extreme south-west to John O'Groats, the north-eastern tip of Scotland. The same company owns both sites, and has even designated an official start and finish line for "end to enders".

Bath

Other than London, Bath is perhaps the city that most completely reflects England's history. In one short walking tour you can visit the Roman Baths (right) which were built at a spring venerated by the Celts, then wander on to Bath Abbey, and later the Royal Crescent. Bath's popularity soared during the Georgian era when some of its most enduring architectural gems were built, such as the Royal Crescent and other fine terraces of townhouses.

The Cotswolds

The warm Cotswold stone is one of the attractions of the towns and villages in these hills. This area of central England prospered from the wool trade in the 15th and 16th centuries, when many cottages, manor houses and churches were built in the local honey-coloured limestone.

Lower Slaughter (below), a typical pretty Cotswold settlement, sits either side of a stream, the Eye. The village's name simply means "wet land" and its beautiful old houses have steeply pitched gables and mullioned windows.

Oxford

Matthew Arnold's often-quoted description of Oxford as "that sweet city with her dreaming spires" still rings true today. The town is dominated by its ancient university, founded in the 12th century, and the colleges jostle close to one another in the centre. Each college is autonomous; many were built around a quadrangle in order to enhance the feeling of community. The Radcliffe Camera (above) was opened in 1749 to house a science library for the university. Today it is a history and English reading room for the Bodleian Library. One of Oxford's largest colleges, Christ Church, is also the cathedral of the city.

Blenheim Palace

Blenheim was named after one of the most important military victories of John Churchill, the first Duke of Marlborough, in 1704. Queen Anne was so grateful that she granted him Woodstock and declared she would build him a house at her own expense. In the event, the Duke had to pay more than £45,000 to finish the work. Blenheim Palace retains a strong flavour of that era.

Marlborough's most illustrious descendant was the statesman, prime minister and author Sir Winston Churchill (1874-1965). After a state funeral he was buried in the graveyard of Bladon Church (right) on the Blenheim estate.

Cambridge

One in five of the population of Cambridge is a student at the university. This ancient seat of learning dates back to the early 13th century, when students fled from violence in Oxford and set up in this small town on the banks of the river Cam. The town has grown up around the classically beautiful buildings of the 31 colleges and their grounds. The façade of King's College Chapel (above) is one of the most beautiful sights of Cambridge. Every year, the Christmas Eve service is broadcast live across the world from its chapel (below). Trinity College is the university's richest college. The college numbers 31 Nobel Laureates among its many illustrious students.

Stratford-upon-Avon

It is hard to ignore the presence of the Great Bard in Stratford. This was after all the birthplace of William Shakespeare (1564–1616), and today it is the home of the Royal Shakespeare Company. The river Avon flows through the town, past the Royal Shakespeare Theatre (right). In front of the theatre are the Bancroft Gardens where a statue of Shakespeare sits with four key figures from his plays: Prince Hal, Falstaff, Lady Macbeth and Hamlet (above). A house on Henley Street is thought to be where Shakespeare was born and spent his childhood. A mile west of Stratford is the village of Shottery and Anne Hathaway's cottage where Shakespeare courted his wife-to-be. This substantial house is timbered, with a low thatched roof and lattice windows.

Norfolk Broads

The shallow lakes and rivers of the Broads are largely manmade, the result of more than 350 years' intensive digging of peat (turf) for fuel. The pits where the peat had been dug away gradually filled with water and by the 14th century the peat could no longer be reached. The land flooded, forming the wetlands known today as the Norfolk and Suffolk Broads. You won't travel far along the waterways before you see a windmill – and then another, built to aid drainage. The river Thurne (above) rises near Martham Broad and joins the river Bure near St Benet's Abbey. The reedbeds in this area are an important habitat for birds.

Warwick Castle

In 1752 Canaletto painted Warwick Castle, serene atop its hillside. It remains arguably the best preserved castle in Britain today. Inside the castle walls, however, its turbulent history becomes clear. This was a castle built to withstand siege and attack. The towers were key to its defence, jutting out above the walls to give archers a clear line of sight sideways and downwards. On the land side stands Guy's Tower (1395), 12-sided and five storeys high. Shaped like a clover-leaf, Caesar's Tower (below) seems to grow out of the rocks above the river Avon. Concealed below is a grim dungeon, a dank hole in which prisoners were left to rot.

Ironbridge

This quiet gorge was the birthplace of the Industrial Revolution. The ground-breaking decision to build a cast-iron bridge across the Severn at Coalbrookdale sprang from Abraham Darby's novel technique of smelting iron with coke rather than charcoal. Suddenly, high-quality iron could be made in vast quantities, affordably and at speed. When the single-span bridge (right) opened in 1781, people came from far and wide to marvel at the structure. The town was so proud that it changed its name to Ironbridge.

The toll-house still stands on the bridge, although today you must cross on foot. It now houses the Ironbridge Tourist Information Centre and one of the area's 10 museums, all celebrating aspects of the area's industrial past.

Manchester

This dynamic cultural and commercial centre is the capital of the north-west and vies with Birmingham for the title of England's second city. The 19th-century Gothic Town Hall and its imposing clock tower (left) loom over Albert Square. Neighbouring Salford has now merged into Manchester. Its resurgence in recent years owes much to its illustrious son, LS Lowry. His paintings of "matchstick" working folk are housed in the ultra-modern Lowry Centre (below) in Salford Quays.

Blackpool

The famous Blackpool Illuminations light up five miles of the seafront every year from September to November. Blackpool Tower (above) was designed in 1894 as a replica of the Eiffel Tower. People flock to take in the shows and go dancing in the ornate ballroom beneath the tower.

Liverpool

In the 1960s Liverpool's reputation soared as the home of the legendary Beatles, Gerry and the Pacemakers and many other bands. The Beatles first made their name at the Cavern Club in Mathew Street. But the city has much to offer beyond the pop scene – two football clubs, the Toffeemen (Everton) and the Reds (Liverpool), its own Philharmonic Orchestra, and the Tate in the North gallery. The city's two cathedrals reflect its strong Protestant and Catholic traditions.

The city's best-known building is the Liver Building, on Pier Head at the mouth of the River Mersey. Its bronze cormorants, the Liver Birds, spread their wings on two towers with the largest clockfaces in Britain. Liverpool has long been Britain's key port for sea trade with North America, from the days of cotton and slave-trading in the 18th century to the busy container port of today.

Chatsworth

Eight miles north of Matlock in the heart of the Peak District stands Chatsworth House (left), the seat of the Duke of Devonshire. This graceful building combines classical architecture with a remarkable natural setting. In an age when we expect instant garden makeovers in a weekend, it is uplifting to see the fulfilment of the vision of Capability Brown, the master landscape designer, 250 years after he set about redesigning the grounds at Chatsworth.

Peak District

Established in 1951, the Peak District was Britain's first national park. This dramatic landscape is noted for its drystone walls, gentle wooded or heather-covered slopes and stark rocky outcrops – and above it all, acres of sky. There is a wealth of pretty villages, including Castleton, together with the spa town of Buxton and the market town of Bakewell. Just eight miles from the heart of Sheffield is Burbage Rocks (below) a typical Peak District landscape.

Yorkshire Dales

Most of Yorkshire's dales are named after their principal river. Hence Swaledale (above) follows the winding river Swale as it runs east from the village of Keld to the market town of Richmond. In the 18th century Swaledale was an important leadmining area, but today it is best known for its sheep and cheese, and of course the dramatic landscape. The Vikings' name for a steep-sided valley, *dael*, is just one of the many echoes of this region's past. Some of the dales are wide and lush, others steep and narrow: all follow the course of their rivers as they head east to the sea.

York

The capital of Roman Britain for some 400 years, York was an important city long before London. In the 9th century the Vikings settled here, naming the town Jorvik.

The city is still dominated by its Gothic cathedral, York Minster (right). In July 1984 it lost its ancient oak roof and some of the stonework in a dramatic fire. Traditional craftsmen have since restored the building to its former glory.

The Shambles is probably the best-known street in the whole of York today. Its half-timbered medieval houses are a major tourist attraction.

Lake District

This is a region of sublime scenery, which includes beautiful lakes and charming villages. Here you will find the highest points in England including the mountains of Scafell and Helvellyn. Visitors often compare the serene beauty of lakes such as Ullswater with Lake Lucerne in Switzerland. Those who prefer more rugged landscapes will appreciate Wast Water (left) further west, with its dramatic scree slopes sweeping down to its eastern shore.

Durham

Under the Normans, Benedictine monks built Durham Cathedral and the nearby Durham Castle. St Cuthbert's shrine ensured that a steady flow of pilgrims kept the cathedral's coffers full. Today Durham Castle, the cathedral and the landlocked island on which they are sited is a World Heritage Site. The author Bill Bryson considers Durham "the best cathedral on Planet Earth". Its soaring nave has been an inspiration to many, and the bell tower houses a magnificent ring of 10 bells.

Angel of the North

Antony Gormley's iconic sculpture, the *Angel of the North* (above) spreads its wings on a hill just outside Gateshead. The public perception of the twin cities of Newcastle and Gateshead, either side of the Tyne, has changed dramatically in the last decade. Now the secret is out: this is a vibrant place, with an important history and stylish contemporary architecture.

Newcastle

Newcastle has a long tradition of radical bridge design. The Tyne Bridge (left), a compression arch suspended-deck bridge, opened in 1928. Beyond is the 19th-century Armstrong Swing Bridge which pivots on a central pier in the river, and beyond that the High Level Bridge. The most recent addition, opened in 2002, is the Gateshead Millennium Bridge which can be "tilted like the opening of an eye" to allow ships to pass upriver.

Lindisfarne

Lindisfarne is known locally as Holy Island. St Aidan founded a monastery here in AD634, a centre of early Christianity. Later that century Bishop Eadfrith and his monks illuminated the incomparable Lindisfarne Gospels in honour of his predecessor St Cuthbert. A century after the Vikings burnt down the monastery in AD793 the monks left the island, taking St Cuthbert's relics and the Lindisfarne Gospels with them. Today Durham Cathedral and the British Museum are custodians of Cuthbert's remains and the Lindisfarne Gospels.

Hadrian's Wall

Hadrian's Wall stretches 73 miles (117km) across from the Solway Firth to the river Tyne and took six years to build, from AD122-128. The Barbarian hordes on the other side would have faced a 15ft-high (4m) stone wall surmounted by another six feet (2m) of timber. Sixteen forts, another 80 mile-castles and many signal turrets ensured speedy communication and reinforcement along the line.

Cardiff

Remarkably green and uncrowded, Cardiff is Europe's youngest capital city. It sits at the mouth of the Taff, Rhymney and Ely rivers and at its heart stands Cardiff Castle, complete with clock tower (left). The living quarters of the castle were given a Gothic makeover in the 1860s.

In the 20th century Cardiff was transformed. City Hall (below) opened when it achieved city status in 1905. Fifty years later Cardiff was proclaimed the capital of the principality, and in 1999 it became home to the Welsh Assembly.

Ultra-modern buildings symbolise the vigour of the city today. The Cardiff Bay Visitor Centre, down by the old coal docks, is known as "the Tube" because of its striking design. In 2004, the Wales Millennium Centre was opened as an exciting new venue for classical music, opera and concerts. Best known of all is the gleaming Millennium Stadium (right) with its retractable roof, which firmly places Cardiff in the international arena for rugby, football and speedway.

Gower Peninsula

When you see the magnificent coastline, it is not surprising to learn that the Gower is the most visited part of Wales after Snowdonia. It is just 16 miles (26km) by seven miles (11km) wide and justifiably classed as an area of outstanding natural beauty. On the southern tip of Swansea Bay lies the village of Mumbles, with its lighthouse and the renowned cluster of pubs where the poet Dylan Thomas used to drink.
Further along the southern coast is Three Cliffs Bay (right), popular with rock climbers. In the far south-west of the peninsula the village of Rhossili perches on cliffs. At low tide you can walk out to the rocky outcrop known as Worm's Head.

Snowdonia

Snowdonia National Park is the backdrop
for much of central and north-west Wales.
Its best-known mountain is the five-
peaked Yr Wyddfa, otherwise known as
Snowdon. At 3,560ft (1,085m), Snowdon
is Wales' highest mountain. It is star-shaped
with six ridges, each fanning out into a
cwm (valley) with its own distinct
character. To the south of Snowdonia the
looming slopes of Cadair Idris dominate
the landscape. Below Cadair Idris are the
Cregennen Lakes (above). The craggy face
of Tyrrau Mawr looms above the waters
and at several points close to the lakes
there are magnificent views of the
Mawddach Estuary, Barmouth and the
distant Lleyn Peninsula.

Harlech

Incredibly it took just seven years to build
the stronghold of Harlech Castle, part
of the iron ring of castles Edward I built
to subdue the Welsh. Harlech has a long
history of siege: if the rocks on its three
land sides failed to hold back the attackers,
then the concentric series of outer and
inner walls and the twin-towered
gatehouse kept them at bay. In 1294 the
Welsh rebel Madog failed, but in 1404
Owain Glyndwr triumphed by securing
the sea approaches, only to lose Harlech
Castle to the English five years later.

Portmeirion

One man's vision became reality when the architect Clough Williams-Ellis created the village of Portmeirion. The project dominated Clough's life from 1925-1976, and the village that you see today is very much as he planned it. It is more Mediterranean than Welsh, with houses painted in whites and pastels and palm trees swaying in the breeze. Some people consider it simply quirky, but Clough's designs incorporate architectural objects salvaged elsewhere into a harmonious whole.

Caernarfon

As with the other castles in the iron ring built by the English King Edward I, Caernarfon Castle (below) was not raised to protect the Welsh but to impose English rule upon them. This is certainly an awe-inspiring fortress, with its octagonal towers and crenellated walls (nine feet thick in some places) but it was not impregnable. In 1294 it was briefly taken by Welsh nationalists, and Cromwell's troops seized it in 1646. Edward I dedicated his infant son here in 1284 as the Prince of Wales; the traditional title passed to the monarch's eldest son but six centuries went by before the next investiture was held at Caernarfon, when, on July 1 1969, HRH Prince Charles the Prince of Wales was invested at Caernarfon Castle.

Menai Strait

The Menai Bridge (above) was designed by engineer Thomas Telford as a link in the important London to Holyhead route for travellers to Ireland. The Menai Bridge you see today is still Telford's design, although much modified since it opened in 1824.

Conwy

One of Edward I's earliest Welsh castles, Conwy, perches on cliffs above the town. Two years after he designed the Menai Bridge, Thomas Telford turned his hand to the much smaller Conwy Suspension Bridge (left) across the river Conwy. Its graceful lines flow from supporting towers that echo the shape of the castle's turrets. Despite a turbulent past, the walled town of Conwy has some interesting buildings including Britain's smallest house and Aberconwy House, which belonged to a 14th-century merchant.

Edinburgh

Edinburgh's Princes Street (below) has something for everyone – fashionable shops; the Princes Street Gardens along the south side, complete with a funfair and ice rink at Christmas; the monument to Scotland's favourite author Sir Walter Scott and his dog. It runs parallel to the famous Royal Mile, which has linked the palace of Holyrood House with Edinburgh Castle since the Middle Ages. Many of Edinburgh's key attractions lie along these two thoroughfares.

From the city's much-loved Calton Hill the panorama sweeps across the Old Town to Edinburgh Castle. Night and day the Castle, perched on its volcanic crag, dominates the city. In August the castle esplanade is packed with 217,000 spectators for the annual Edinburgh Military Tattoo (above): massed pipes and drums vie with military marching bands and Highland dancers, and in the closing moments a lone piper plays a lament on the castle ramparts.

Forth Bridge

The huge structure of the Forth Railway Bridge – its central span is over 1,100 yards (1km) long – inevitably required continuous maintenance, and "painting the Forth Bridge" became a metaphor for an endless (and unrewarding) task. But new technology now means it will only need to be repainted every 30 years. The new road bridge opened in 1964 stands behind the rail bridge.

Glasgow

Since 1990, when it was the European City of Culture, Glasgow has become a major player on the culture trail and is now a vibrant international centre. Kelvingrove Art Gallery and Museum (right) is Glasgow's favourite Edwardian building, and the most visited museum in the UK outside London. The building itself is in a Spanish Baroque style, and its wide-ranging collections include major Impressionist paintings. At the heart of the city is George Square (below) with statues of Scotland's greats including Robert Burns, James Watt and Sir Walter Scott. The river Clyde, once the key to the city's commercial prominence, is now home to the Science Centre and the Scottish Exhibition Centre.

Stirling

The childhood home of Mary Queen of Scots, Stirling (above) is the grandest castle in Scotland. It looms over the scene of some of the nation's most important battles and the castle was frequently besieged as England fought to dominate the Scottish kingdom. In 1297 William Wallace triumphed over Edward I's army at Stirling Bridge. Seventeen years later the English were once again defeated by Robert the Bruce at Bannockburn.

St Andrews

The ruins of St Andrews Cathedral (right) bear witness to St Andrews' medieval origins. St Andrews University is the third oldest in Britain, dating from 1410.
Golfers everywhere consider St Andrews as the home of their sport. For more than 250 years the Royal and Ancient Golf Club has been the arbiter of the rules of golf. On the 18th fairway of the Old Course, golfers cross the Old Swilken Bridge as they near the clubhouse.

Loch Lomond

Twenty miles north-west of Glasgow, across the Kilpatrick Hills, lies Scotland's most famous loch. The tranquil, cold waters of Loch Lomond run 600ft (196m) deep in places. This is the UK's largest freshwater loch, 24 miles long and five miles wide (38km by 8km). Most visitors will hope to catch the classic view of the loch's mirror-like waters reflecting the snow-capped peak of Ben Lomond (left), from the pier in the village of Luss. Although the mountain qualifies as a Munro (a peak over 3,000ft/914m), serious climbers are disdainful of the easy trek to the summit. On a clear day, however, the views over the loch and Southern Highlands are enough to raise the spirits of the most hardened cynic.

Glen Coe

If you are walking the challenging West Highland Way, you come to the wilds of Rannoch Moor (below) with its rocks, lochs and mountains – here you see Ba Loch with Black Mount in the background. Where Glen Etive meets the pass of Glen Coe, Stob Dearg (top of photograph) rises at the end of the Buachaille Etive Mor ridge. This peak is a favourite with walkers and climbers of all abilities.

Many people still feel a frisson as they enter Glen Coe, an echo of the horrific massacre of the Clan MacDonald in January 1692. The MacDonalds had given their traditional rivals, the Campbells, shelter for 10 days before their guests turned on them on the order of King William III. Many of those who escaped died of hunger and exposure in the surrounding hills. Today Glen Coe is promoted as "the cradle of Scottish mountaineering".

Loch Ness

You will probably not spot the legendary monster in the beautiful waters of Loch Ness that stretch from Inverness to Fort Augustus, but you are certain to see a rich variety of birds – if you are lucky you may even see an osprey fishing for salmon or brown trout.

By Drumnadrochit on the north bank, the ruins of Castle Urquhart sit on Strone Point (below). This used to be the largest of all Scotland's castles: it was much enlarged by the English King Edward I. In his continuing efforts to subdue the country he became known as the Hammer of the Scots.

The Caledonian Canal links Loch Ness with Loch Oich and Loch Lochy to the south. Opened in 1822 it created a waterway from Fort William in the west to Inverness in the east – a short-cut between the North Sea and the Atlantic Ocean.

First published in 2009 by Myriad Books Limited
35 Bishopsthorpe Road, London SE26 4PA

Photographs copyright © Britain on View,
the image resource centre of Visit Britain

Text copyright © Lisa Pritchard

ISBN 1 84746 249 9

Designed by Jerry Goldie Graphic Design

Printed in China

www.myriadbooks.com